CHURCHTOWN IN CAMERA

EARLY PHOTOGRAPHS, INCLUDING MARSHSIDE & CROSSENS

•

by

Andrew Farthing

SEFTON
LIBRARIES

Uniform with this volume:
Crosby in Camera: early photographs of Great Crosby & Waterloo
Seaforth in Camera: early photographs of the district once known as Litherland Marsh

1999
Published by
Sefton Council
Leisure Services Department (Libraries)
Pavilion Buildings, 99-105 Lord Street
Southport PR8 1RH

ISBN 1-874516-06-5

Printed in Great Britain
by
Mitchell & Wright Printers Ltd

INTRODUCTION

This album contains fifty pictures of old Churchtown, Crossens and Marshside. Most scenes pre-date the Second World War and show the communities when they were relatively isolated from Southport town.

The selection has been made from the extensive local history collection at Southport Library and loans from organisations and members of the public. The breadth of Southport's photograph collection owes much to the dedication and expertise of the former librarians. Also the generosity of residents, local societies, the Botanic Gardens Museum, the Southport Visiter and expatriates, has enriched the collection with postcards, family snaps, topical scenes and local views. The collection, built up over many years, continues to grow. It is a storehouse of the area's visual history - and a freely accessible gateway to local studies.

Invariably, however, many aspects of life do not figure in this album. The physical condition of some photographs has prevented reproduction; and the library's collection lacks photographs of certain local buildings, events and personalities. Nonetheless, what follows may serve for many people as an introduction to the history of these three communities; for others it will be a reminder of times past.

In order to assist readers in locating the site or viewpoint of photographs, an early map is located at the back of the book. A guide to further reading and a list of the photographs are also included.

ANF
October 1999

ACKNOWLEDGEMENTS

As a relative newcomer to the Churchtown area I have relied heavily on the many past historical works about the area for much background information. Some of the photos included here have been reproduced in older books, but many have never been published before. Most of the information about the photos has been obtained from the local history collection in Southport Library. Some of the more obscure or personal details have been contributed by members of the public, a number of whom have also kindly loaned photos for use in this book. For such help I am extremely grateful to Phil Coghlin of the Southport Visiter, Harold Crosdale, Audrey Garlick, Jack Harris, Robert Hesketh, Leonard Lloyd, Miss M. Nutter, David Pearson, Tom Rimmer, Ken Wighthead, W.Wignall and Joyce Wright. Two organisations have also supplied unstinting support: the Birkdale and Ainsdale Historical Research Society has supplied rare photos and much information about Marshside; Jo Jones, Acting Keeper of Galleries and Museums, based at the Botanic Gardens Museum, Churchtown, has loaned material and given advice. Thanks must go to my colleagues in Sefton Library Service - Jenny Stanistreet, Matthew Tinker, Richard Hall; also to the staff at Churchtown Library whose hard work, enthusiasm and local knowledge is second to none.

1

Churchtown Village.

This contemporary sketch of Churchtown in 1853 shows a very rural picture of the village. At the time Churchtown only had three named lanes, Mill Lane, Marshside Lane and `Rowe' Lane, though there were various unnamed thoroughfares. However, even by the 1850s, it could boast two schools, the National School and a boarding school on `Rowe' Lane.

3.
Mill Lane

Now the top end of Mill Lane, originally this stretch of road was part of Roe Lane. The residents of Mill Lane were a cross section of local society. The well-to-do lived on the left side of the lane in houses such as Brooklyn Villa, Rusher House and Clifton Lodge. Those on the right side were less genteel, making their living as carters, labourers or dairymen.

2.
Wounded Soldiers on Roe Lane

The Grange Hospital was set up in 1915 to alleviate the shortage of bed space for soldiers wounded in the First World War. Loaned by Major Fleetwood-Hesketh, 'The Grange' stood on the corner of Grange Road and Roe Lane and became the largest St John's Voluntary Aid Detachment Hospital in Britain, with 6887 patients admitted. To relieve the soldiers' boredom entertainment was organised, including drives round the local area such as the one shown here beginning on Roe Lane.

4.
The Old Mill

Churchtown Mill was built in 1725 and situated in Mill Lane, approximately where No.32 Mill Lane is now. It was a flour grinding mill driven by wind power, but in 1856 a steam engine was installed and in 1861 the sails were removed. A fire about fifteen years later led to the demolition of the tower and the mill was rebuilt. By 1928 diesel had replaced steam power, but in 1955 it finally closed.

6.
Lloyd Family of Peets Farm

The owners of Peets Farm, the Lloyd family, are pictured in front of the property on Peets Lane c1903. The mother of the family (sitting) is Mary Jane, a member of the Peet family, the original owners of the farm. The Peets were one of the oldest local families and Peets Lane was named after them in the early 1890s.

5.
Cottages on Botanic Road

This is one of the earliest cottages in the whole of Southport. The roof timbers are evidently from an old sailing ship; they have been recycled to build the cottage. This was the home of the Hunt family for several generations. Robert Hunt, a bricklayer by trade, was born in the cottage in 1842 and died there in 1918. He was known as `Owd Tune' Hunt because he was often found playing a penny whistle outside the house. At one time silk weaving took place in one of the upstairs rooms.

7 & 8.

Alice Johnson

Alice Johnson is pictured here in younger days as the epitome of Edwardian gentility. In 1914 she took over the shop at 92 Botanic Road which she ran as the village stationers and newsagents. She later diversified to selling fancy goods. After 40 years running her business in Churchtown, Miss Johnson died in November 1951 and was buried in St Cuthbert's Churchyard. Amazingly the building is still a newsagents today.

10.
The Farmers Arms

Built in 1841 this house had an early history in the brewing trade. In 1876 Nathan Threlfall and William Ball ran their separate beerselling businesses from the house. By 1881 Alice Threlfall and Jane Ball had taken over the respective firms. In 1890 William Birchall set up his beerselling business on the premises and under him it became the Farmers Arms. The pub was forced to close in September 1935 by Southport Corporation.

9.
Cottages on Botanic Road

The community at the St Cuthbert's end of Botanic Road in 1910 boasted a fish & chip shop, shoe maker, hairdresser, grocer, confectioner and tailor. The building in the photo is now an antique shop, but was then private apartments.

12.
The Hesketh Arms

The Hesketh Arms was originally called `The Black Bull' but changed its name around the same time as the Bold Arms. Like the Bold, the Hesketh Arms was named after one of the local manorial families, the Heskeths of Meols Hall. One famous innkeeper of `The Black Bull' was William Sutton, considered the founder of Southport.

11.
The Bold Arms Hotel c1895.

First recorded in 1637, the original ale house consisted of what is now the public bar. The lounge was converted from two old cottages and the restaurant from further cottages. Originally called `The Griffin', by 1848 the pub had been renamed the Bold Arms after the Bold Family. Their crest can still be seen above the fireplace.

14.

Johnson's Garage, Cambridge Road.
This early photo shows William 'Tag' Johnson hand pumping petrol. This family-run firm has been on the site since 1898 when 'Tag' Johnson set himself up as a cycle builder. He developed the business to include various aspects of the motor trade and this proved successful. The firm is still there.

13.

Marshside Road & Cambridge Road c1905.
Trams and the railway were to dramatically change society in this area. About ten years before this picture was taken the immediate community was very rural with labourers, fishermen, cowkeepers, hawkers and shrimp dealers living there. Within ten years of the photo being taken, however, more prosperous folk had moved in pushing the traditional local families ever northwards. Preston New Road, built in the 1930s, is now just beyond the houses on the right of the picture.

15.
Churchtown Station

The opening of the railway line to Churchtown and Crossens was to have a profound effect. Together with the new tram routes it allowed greater access to Southport for commuters; thus housing developments increased. Churchtown Station was on Cambridge Road where the medical centre is today.

16.
Horse-Drawn tram

The Churchtown horse-drawn tram is pictured outside the Park Hotel, Birkdale. The first horse-drawn tramway was opened in May 1873 by the Southport Tramway Company and ran from Birkdale to the Botanic Gardens. In 1896 the company sold the lines to Southport Corporation and subsequently leased them back off their new owners for 21 years from 1901.

17.
Electrification of tram lines

In 1900 construction of the new electrified routes began. The photo shows the inaugural ceremony of the route on 18th July 1900. The line opened in August 1901 when trams ran from Botanic Gardens to Lord Street via Cambridge Road. An alternative line from Lord Street to Botanic Gardens via Roe Lane opened a month later. Through fares from Birkdale to Churchtown were 3d on the outside top deck and 4d inside. A minimum fare of 2d applied.

18.

St Cuthbert's Church in 1895

The present St Cuthbert's Church dates from 1571, though there has been a church on the site since Norman times. The greater part of St Cuthbert's was rebuilt in 1730 and about nine years later the present tower and spire were added. The church building underwent a major conversion in 1909, with an extension to the rear, a porch and a roof window being added. The ground on which the church stands has evidently been submerged by the sea. When digging graves, layers of sea shells several inches thick have been found at a depth of 3 or 4 feet below the surface.

20.
The Independent Chapel
The Independent Chapel was opened in 1807 at a cost of £70 to build. It could seat up to 200 people. In 1831 the building was replaced by a larger chapel situated in the area known as Off Botanic Road.

19.
Churchtown National School Children
There has been a school at Churchtown since 1684 when the first grammar school was founded. In 1826 this school was converted into Churchtown National School. This building is now the Conservative Club next to St Cuthbert's Church. In 1859 a much larger school was erected at a cost of £2200. When Southport Corporation took over the running of the school in 1911, it was rebuilt again and became known as Southport Churchtown School.

21. Meols Hall

22. A portrait of Sir Peter Fleetwood-Hesketh, M.P and his daughter Anna Maria in 1839.

23. Reverend Charles Hesketh

Meols Hall's history has been as turbulent as that of its owners, the Hesketh family. The Heskeths have been (joint) Lords of the Manor since the 16th century, when a huge house was built on the site. In 1733 the family moved to Rossall Hall and a large part of Meols Hall was demolished. The remainder was occupied by the Hesketh's agent until 1840 when it became a farmhouse. In the Great War the hall became a military hospital and the Heskeths returned in 1919. The present hall was dramatically redesigned between 1960-64 by Colonel Roger Hesketh.

Two of the more well known members of the family are Sir Peter Fleetwood-Hesketh and the Rev. Charles Hesketh. Sir Peter is famous for the founding and development of the town of Fleetwood, an enterprise which nearly bankrupted him. In 1840 he was forced to open negotiations with Charles Scarisbrick to buy his North Meols property to clear his debts and provide further capital. His brother Rev. Charles Hesketh was so keen to keep

Meols Hall that he offered a higher price of £148,000 for it. This was duly accepted.

Rev. Charles Hesketh was born in 1804 and became the minister of St Cuthbert's Church in 1835. The new incumbent set about his duties with such energy that one contemporary described his success as "a new and surprising revolution". He was also a shrewd business man. He gave undeveloped and sandy land to the local authority to make into a park, which they duly did, creating Hesketh Park. Charles Hesketh had retained ownership of the land round the new park and this now became a prime real estate site. He died in 1876 after 41 years service and we are told that the whole parish mourned.

24.

Botanic Gardens

The Botanic Gardens were built on the site of an earlier smaller park known as Churchtown Strawberry Gardens. Opened in 1875 as a private venture, it was owned and run by the Churchtown Botanic Gardens & Museum Company. The museum was opened a year later along with the conservatory and refreshment rooms. After a long period of success the company went bankrupt in 1932. To pay its creditors the museum stock was auctioned off. The sale horrified many local people and a campaign was started to re-open the museum. In 1937 Southport Corporation took over the business and ran it until 1974 when Sefton Council assumed the responsibility. In World War II, the Botanic Gardens were the base for the US Army Medical Corps, who converted the café into a temporary cinema.

25.

Conservatory, Botanic Gardens

The site of the Botanic Gardens was one of the first local areas to be enclosed from the sea. After its enclosure, shipwrecks were found in the grounds. The stream is thought once to have been a river known as Otterspool. Legend has it that the Vikings rowed up this river and founded Crossens.

26.
Crossens Festival 1914
The Crossens Festival was the highlight of the year for many. First held in 1906, it was founded by the members of St John's Church. Initially the Rose Queen was crowned on the second day of the Horticultural Show, but after a while the event became a festival in its own right. In 1952 the church relinquished its control of the festival to the education authority.

28.
Rufford Road

This shop on the corner of Rufford Road and Land Lane was run by Mr & Mrs Johnson. The photo of Mrs Johnson standing in the doorway dates from about 1913. Mr Johnson had, two years earlier, run a stall at the Pleasureland. When the shop was sold he became a commercial traveller while Mrs Johnson brought up the children. The photo highlights the Methodist influence in the area: temperance drinks are on sale. The shop is still a newsagents today.

27.
Crossens Festival 1912

This was the last time that the Rose Queen rode a horse in the parade. The queen, Elsie Cropper (centre) was thrown to the ground when the horse reared after being touched by the feather of a hat. After this incident, the Rose Queens travelled in a carriage. The Goodrich Tyres sign on the left is where the entrance to Drewitt Close now stands.

30.
Crossens Festival c1925
Along with the Rose Queen, one of the regular features of the Crossens Festival was the representation of the four seasons. Each season had a `Queen' and a train of followers. The photo shows the Winter Queen, who wore a dark red cloak and winter foliage.

29.
'Ideal Laundry' Van
The Ideal Laundry was based at Crossens, its location being described as "several hundred yards from the centre of the village". In fact it was in Brook Street. Vans like this collected laundry daily throughout Southport. The laundry flourished from about 1912 until the late 1960's.

31.
Rufford Road 1919

The long arm of the law was never far away even on Festival day. From 1870, Southport had its own police force until it merged with the Lancashire Constabulary in 1969. At the time of this photo the force was just recovering its strength. Over 49 of the 103 police officers had left for service in the First World War and those who had survived were just returning.

32.

St John's Church

The first St John's Church was constructed in 1837 and used the same design as Holy Trinity Church, Southport. In 1860, the separate parish of Crossens was carved out of the old parish of St Cuthbert's. By the 1880s, the parishioners had outgrown the church so the incumbent, Rev. William Bulpit, obtained money to build a larger structure. Costing £3120, the new church was consecrated in 1885. Construction had its problems when the planned spire had to be taken down, leaving the church as it is today.

33.

The Crossens Canoe

The Reverend Bulpit, vicar of St John's Church, was a keen local historian. On 22nd April 1899, one of his parishioners, Peter Brookfield, was ploughing a field when his plough struck something hard. Closer examination revealed a wooden object with an antiquated look. Bulpit was called to the scene and identified it as a dugout canoe of early origin, though strangely a musket was found in it and metal sheets had been riveted to the side. Bulpit sent a cart to transport the canoe to a safer location but the farmer's wife had locked the gates and was demanding £50. Bulpit gave her "a present of a couple of guineas" and the canoe was moved. It was exhibited round the borough, including at the Botanic Gardens Museum, where it is still on display. Recent carbon dating of the canoe has arrived at a date of 535AD.

35.
The Vulcan Motor Company

The Vulcan Motor Company, Crossens, was founded by Thomas and Joseph Hampson in 1891 in a building on Yellow House Lane. By 1907 the company had moved to this new factory at Crossens which at its height employed 700 workers. In the First World War, production of cars was suspended and the company concentrated on lorries and ambulances, manufacturing over 1000 lorries alone in the war years.

34.
Crossens Station

The first sod of the Southport to Preston line was cut in 1873. However the new West Lancashire Railway Company, which was building the line, soon experienced financial difficulties due to the excessive cost of the project. It was only saved by the intervention of Edward Holden, owner of the Southport Daily News, who invested in the firm and became its chairman. The first stretch of line, including stations at Churchtown and Crossens (shown here in 1955), was opened in February 1878. The line was eventually completed 4 years later but was never successful and was finally bought by the Lancashire & Yorkshire Railway in 1897. It continued to struggle but eventually closed in September 1964 as part of major cuts in the national railway network.

36.
The Vulcan Motor Company

In 1917 Thomas Hampson of the Vulcan Motor Company became Southport's first Roman Catholic mayor. However, two years later he suddenly retired from the firm. Financial irregularities soon began to surface and he was eventually sentenced to 12 months in prison. In 1922 Vulcan began producing work for Lea-Francis of Coventry, but by 1928 car production had ceased at Crossens, with the firm concentrating on commercial vehicles. In 1931 a court order wound up the company. The right to build Vulcan vehicles was bought by Tillings Stevens and the factory building was sold to Brockhouse Engineering Company.

37.

The Plough Hotel

Morris dancers from St John's School are seen here in front of the Plough Hotel in 1908. There was a hierarchy at the school for the Crossens Festival. Young pupils started off holding the maypole; as they grew older they wore the fancy dress costumes; and the oldest boys became morris dancers and sword dancers. The old school (to the left of the picture) was pulled down in the 1950s and the site was used as a tradesman's yard.

38.

A Marshside Shrimper

This Marshside shrimper is posing outside his house (probably on Shellfield Road) with his equipment on display. With his waders, net and basket, shrimpers of this type were known as 'putters' after their technique of shrimping. They waded through the water pushing their nets in front and scooping the shrimps out. Just behind the shrimper is a birdcage. Song birds were often caught and sold by the fishermen to supplement their income.

40.
Marshside Carnival
An annual event, the Marshside Carnival, was held on May Day. It was appropriate that the carnival was distinctly fishing-orientated. The procession was led by the King and Queen of the Shrimpers and the maypole was made up of 3 boats' masts lashed together.

39.
Cockling off Marshside
Although this photo of cocklers about 1895 was probably taken on the Marshside coast, the fisherfolk are likely to be from Banks. The cockling industry flourished along the whole local coast. One early cockler, Richard Aughton, is believed to have given his name to Cockle Dick's Lane. There were no permanent cockle gatherers in Marshside. They only sought cockles when the shrimps were out of season. The cockling industry was very important to the communities of Little Ireland and Banks, but the Marshside shrimpers considered themselves to be a 'cut above' the cocklers. When the cockles had been gathered they were washed in pools which sometimes formed around shipwrecks. Two such pools were Bank Hole, near Bank Nook and Kent's Hole which is now the site of Stanley High School.

41.

Fishermen's Strike 1913

In 1913 the local shrimp industry was in crisis. A harsh winter and an influx of cheap foreign imports left fishermen with little or no work. They decided that enough was enough and on 22nd May 1913 they went on strike and no boats sailed. Ugly scenes arose when a consignment of non-local shrimps arrived at Churchtown Station. The fishermen attacked the cart carrying the shrimps and overturned it. A subsequent consignment received police protection and this led to 29 fishermen being arrested. The photo shows the arrested shrimpers marching through the streets in protest on their way to court.

43.
Delivery Cart in Marshside

In the years before cars and trucks took control, horse power was still the best way for businessmen to deliver their goods to the Southport shops. This picture c1911 shows the cart of James Lloyd and Son, grocers and bakers, of 60 Lytham Road. It was only after World War I that the traditional horse began to be replaced by motor transport.

42.
Marshside Temperance Band

Members of the Marshside Temperance Band, Crossens, are pictured opposite St John's Church. The temperance movement had a great following in Marshside and when the Temperance Hall was opened in 1864 it became the centre of local activities.

44.

Grocers on Marshside Road

This picture of Ball & Son, the grocery store in Marshside Road, was probably taken around 1902 when the business was opened. In 1912 it became Thomas Ball, grocer and provision merchant, and remained so until World War II. Around this time the shop was sold, though it remained a grocers. Originally 88 Marshside Road, the house number, in common with many in Southport, was changed as more houses were built. In 1924 it became 118 Marshside Road and it retains its grocery connection today as Bob's Corner Market.

Shellfield Road

Shellfield Road, as the name suggests, has had maritime connections. At the turn of the century, common occupations of those who lived there were fisherman, shrimp dealer and labourer. At the time of this photo, about 1927, of the 123 houses on Shellfield Road, 24 were occupied by people involved in the fishing industry.

45.

Post Office on Marshside Road

Originally numbered 1 Shellfield Road, this building has been a Post Office Receiving House and grocers since the 1880s. Richard Latham took over the business in 1890 and he developed many side-lines. At different times, as well as the postal business, he was a grocer, baker, general dealer and even boatbuilder. The business changed hands sometime during World War I but Robert continued to live there until 1922. The building has been renumbered 3 times, starting as 1 Shellfield Road, then in 1887 becoming 72 Marshside Road, and finally in 1924 it became 100 Marshside Road.

47. Bakery, Marshside Road

Now a private house, 47 Marshside Road had a long history as a grocers, confectioners and bakers from 1924 until the 1970s. Originally farmland up to the 1900s, the land probably belonged to Brickhouse Farm on Marshside Road.

48.

Marshside Methodist Church

Marshside Road Methodist Church was built in 1878 and replaced a smaller building which had been on the site since 1832. The present church was designed by Mr R. Owen, a Liverpool architect. It cost £1864, a princely sum, that was raised by the 'local widows and poor folk' of the area.

49.

31 Cambridge Road.

This fisherman's cottage stood at the corner of Hesketh Road and Cambridge Road until it was demolished in 1932 to make way for modern housing. At the time it was the home of George and Annie Sinclair. Annie, we assume, is the woman in the photograph. This shows the distinctive design of the local fisherman's cottage.

50. Westward

This was one of a group of fishermen's cottages on Cambridge Road (numbers 23-29) called `Westward'. The woman holding the bucket is Martha Watkinson and, from the net, this is obviously a shrimping family. A comparison between this cottage and the Sinclairs' Cottage (previous photo), shows they are almost identical in design. Cottages of this type can still be found in the area and are a signpost to its rural past.

FURTHER READING

This is a representative sample of material relating to the topics covered in the book and to the pre-Second World War history of the Churchtown area. All items listed are available for consultation in the Local History Unit at Southport Library. Readers may wish to pursue particular lines of enquiry beyond the limitations of this list: Sefton's Local History Librarians would be pleased to advise.

Alsop, W.   Concise history of Southport. 1832

Ashton, W.   Evolution of a coastline. 1920

Atkinson, D.   Sand Dunes of the Sefton Coast. 1993

Aughton, P   North Meols & Southport: a history. 1988

Bailey, F. A.   A history of Southport. 1956

Baines, E.   History of the County Palatine of Lancaster. 1836

Bland, E.   Annals of Southport and district: a chronological history of North Meols. 1903

Bulpit, W. T.   Notes on Southport and district. 1908

Burgess, G.A.   Southport through the letterbox. 1990

Cotterall, J.   The West Lancashire Railway. 1982

Dyer, P.R.   A visitors guide to Churchtown. 1977

Farrer, W.   A history of the parish of North Meols. 1903

"   Victoria history of the county of Lancashire. 1907

Farthing, A.   Essential history of Churchtown. 1998

Foster, H.   Southport: A pictorial history. 1995

"   Don e want ony srimps? 1998

Glazebrook,H.   A guide to Southport. 1809 & 1826

Greenwood, C.   Thatch, towers and colonnades: the story of architecture in Southport. 1990.

Gresswell, R.K.   Sandy shores of South Lancashire. 1953

Mannex, P.   History, topography and directory of mid-Lancashire. 1854

Mayer, P.   Southport: a portrait in old picture postcards. 1989

-                  New illustrated guide to Southport. 1876

Parry, K.   Resorts of the Lancashire Coast. 1983

Robinson, F.W.   A descriptive history of the popular watering place of Southport. 1848.

Rothwell, C.   Southport in times past. 1988

Scholes, J.   Churchtown in the parish of North Meols. 1956

Sefton MBC   The Churchtown Village Trail (nd)

Simpson, I.   Southport. 1996

-                  Southport Offical Guide 1908 - 97 (various dates)

Southport Visiter. 1844 - date (microfilm)

Smith, J.   Southport.1995

-                  Stephenson's guide to Southport. 1897-1932

-                  'Visiter' illustrated guide to Southport. 1937 - 67

Warne, F.   Southport: illustrative descriptive history. 1901

GUIDE TO THE ILLUSTRATIONS

Many of the photographs have been loaned specially for this book. We acknowledge the provenance of these items with grateful thanks. Sefton Libraries welcome donations of local photographs - street scenes, church groups, school events, village festivals, people at work, etc. Today's picture is tomorrow's archive! For further information contact the Local History Unit at Southport Library, Lord Street, Southport PR8 1DJ. Telephone: 0151 934 2119.

1. Churchtown Village . *Sefton Libraries*
2. Wounded Soldiers on Roe Lane. *Sefton Libraries*
3. Mill Lane. *Sefton Libraries*
4. The Old Mill. *Sefton Libraries*
5. Cottages on Botanic Road. *Sefton Libraries*
6. Lloyd Family of Peets Farm. *David Pearson Collection*
7. Alice Johnson. *Joyce Wright Collection*
8. Alice Johnson. *Joyce Wright Collection*
9. Cottages on Botanic Road. *Birkdale and Ainsdale Historical Research Society*
10. The Farmers Arms. *Southport Visiter Group*
11. The Bold Arms Hotel. *Birkdale and Ainsdale Historical Research Society*
12. The Hesketh Arms. *Birkdale and Ainsdale Historical Research Society*
13. Marshside Road & Cambridge Road. *Botanic Gardens Museum*
14. Johnson's Garage, Cambridge Road. *Sefton Libraries*
15. Churchtown Station. *Birkdale and Ainsdale Historical Research Society*
16. Horse-Drawn Tram. *Sefton Libraries (P30/17)*
17. Electrification of tram lines. *Sefton Libraries*
18. St Cuthbert's Church. *Sefton Libraries*
19. Churchtown National School Children. *Botanic Gardens Museum*
20. The Independent Chapel. *Botanic Gardens Museum*
21. Meols Hall. *Sefton Libraries (P22/130)*
22. Sir Peter Fleetwood-Hesketh. *Sefton Libraries, with permission of Robert Hesketh*
23. Reverend Charles Hesketh. *Sefton Libraries (S942.72 FAR)*
24. Botanic Gardens. *Botanic Gardens Museum*
25. Conservatory, Botanic Gardens. *Sefton Libraries*
26. Crossens Festival 1914. *Sefton Libraries*
27. Crossens Festival 1912. *Sefton Libraries*
28. Shop on Rufford Road. *Audrey Spencer Collection*
29. Ideal Laundry Van. *Sefton Libraries (S914.272)*
30. Crossens Festival. *Sefton Libraries*
31. Rufford Road in 1919. *Sefton Libraries*
32. St John's Church. *Maud Nutter Collection*
33. The Crossens Canoe. *Botanic Gardens Museum*
34. Crossens Station. *Sefton Libraries*
35. The Vulcan Motor Company. *Botanic Gardens Museum*
36. The Vulcan Motor Company. *Botanic Gardens Museum*
37. The Plough Hotel. *Sefton Libraries*
38. A Marshside Shrimper. *Sefton Libraries (P14/2)*
39. Cocklers off Marshside. *Sefton Libraries (P4/33)*
40. Marshside Carnival. *Birkdale and Ainsdale Historical Research Society*
41. Fishermen's Strike 1913. *Birkdale and Ainsdale Historical Research Society*
42. Marshside Temperance Band. *Birkdale and Ainsdale Historical Research Society*
43. Delivery Cart in Marshside. *Birkdale and Ainsdale Historical Research Society*
44. Grocers on Marshside Road. *Birkdale and Ainsdale Historical Research Society*
45. Post Office on Marshside Road. *Birkdale and Ainsdale Historical Research Society*
46. Shellfield Road. *Sefton Libraries*
47. Bakery, Marshside Road. *Birkdale and Ainsdale Historical Research Society*
48. Marshside Methodist Church. *Birkdale and Ainsdale Historical Research Society*
49. 31 Cambridge Road. *Sefton Libraries*
50. Westward. *Sefton Libraries*